Royal Botanic Gardens Kew | ALYS FOWLER

Grow Forage and Make

illustrated by
HEIDI GRIFFITHS

BLOOMSBURY

Disclaimer
While every effort has been made to ensure the accuracy of the information contained in this book, in no circumstances can the publisher or the author accept any legal responsibility or liability for any loss or damage (including damage to property and/or personal injury) arising from any error in or omission from any information contained in this book, or from the failure of the reader to properly and accurately follow any instructions contained in the book.

Contents

Welcome to the Wonderful World of Plants! 4
How to Use This Book 6
Gardening Equipment 8
Seed Starting Guide for Growing Plants 10
Grow Your Own Tomato Plant 12
Foraging for Leaves that Taste Wild 16
FLOWERS 18
Make a Home for Minibeasts 20
Grow Your Own Lunch 22
Make Your Own Flower Perfume 24
Grow an Air Plant 26
Grow a New Succulent from Leaves 28
Grow Your Own Avocado Tree 30
Make Your Own Plant Labels 33
SEEDS 34
How Plants Take Up Water 36
Edible Flowers 38
Grow Your Own Edible Flowers 40
Edible Flower Recipes: Dandelion Pancakes 42
Edible Flower Recipes: Orange Cheese Sauce 43
LEAVES 44
Make Your Own Plant Pot 46
How to Make Wildflower Seed Paper 48

Making Your Own Vegetable Ink Dye 50
Foraging for Roots that Taste Wild 52
THE NIGHT GARDEN 56
Flowers for Moths 58
Make Your Own Watering Can 61
Grow Your Own Parsnip Pea-Shooter 62
Stems That Play Tricks 65
How to Make a Hoverfly Happy 66
Harvesting your Coriander Seeds 68
How to Taste Nectar 69
ROOTS 70
Making Art with Leaf Pounding 72
Growing a Sweet Potato 74
How to Make a Butterfly Happy 76
How to sow Butterfly Seeds 78
How to Help a Bumblebee 79
Grow Your Own Lentil Farm 80
Growing Microgreens 82
See the Wood Wide Web 84
How to be a Bee 86
STEMS 88
Using Kitchen Scraps to Grow New Plants 90
How to Make a Willow Star Wand 92

Welcome to the Wonderful World of Plants!

I started gardening before I could even ride a bike. I was very small and so was my garden. It was under a fig tree and my mum gave me lots of plants that were lovely to stroke, like Jerusalem sage and lamb's ear. I used to climb the fig tree and look down on my beautiful soft green patch of garden. From then on I was hooked – all I wanted to do was be around plants.

I grew a bit and so did my garden, until eventually I was big enough to go to Kew Gardens to study plants. Now all my days are spent with plants, learning about them, tending to them, coaxing them to grow this way and that and, most importantly, eating some of them!

My life with plants has taken me round the world and now I've collected all this knowledge, distilled it, boiled it up and sprinkled in some joy to create a book full of fun activities that will help you really get to know plants: what they like to do, what they like to drink and how they make their way in the world, as well as some of the many funny and marvellous things they can do.

In this book there are a variety of growing activities that will take anywhere from a few days to a few weeks, as well as some that will last you all summer and beyond – such as growing your own tomato plant or parsnip pea-shooter. Then there are easy and quick foraging activities where you get to taste magical plants that change flavour as you chew (that is, if you're brave enough to try them!). You'll also find plenty of arts and craft activities and even some plant-related experiments!

If you get hooked you might want to go to a garden centre to start your own gardening toolkit, but you can also just reuse lots of things from your recycling and grow stuff from your kitchen cupboard, spice rack and fruit bowl. That's the joy of gardening, it doesn't have to be expensive; a big old kitchen spoon is as good as a trowel for digging and a recycled yoghurt pot makes an excellent growing container. Don't worry if you don't have your own garden either – you can grow most of the plants in this book on the kitchen table, in a pot outside the front door, on a balcony or even on your bedroom windowsill. Or maybe you could try growing some of them in your school garden with your friends.

All of these activities will teach you how to keep your plants happy and well fed, which in turn will mean you'll keep the bees, butterflies and many other insects happy too. When the plants around you are taken care of then the **whole world grows a little better.**

Alys Fowler

How to Use This Book

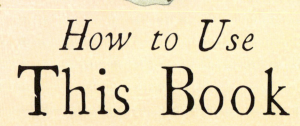

The book is made up of growing, foraging and fun creative activities, experiments, recipes and more! You can go through them in any order or pick and choose the ones that appeal most to you.

For each of the activities, I've given a list of equipment you will need and step-by-step instructions for you to follow. A number of them require some basic bits of equipment, such as plant pots, seed trays, watering cans and labels, and I've suggested ways you can make these from recycled items. Some activities require things that you will need to ask an adult for, such as seeds, food colouring or particular gardening tools. Speak to your adult to see if they might already have things you can use in the kitchen cupboard or garden shed. You should be able to do most of these projects without having to buy anything.

If you find you do need to buy one or two things, like the air plants on p.26 or a bag of compost, you can get these cheaply from your local garden centre or nursery, or even online – just make sure to ask your adult to help you with this.

For a few of the activities, such as the edible flower recipes and making your own wildflower seed paper, you'll need to ask your adult to help with some of the trickier steps. These are marked clearly with a bee sign like this:

I've used a few gardening terms throughout the book that you may not have heard before so I've included an explanation for each of them below:

Sow seeds thickly means that you need to plant LOTS of seeds together. You don't want your seeds to be lonely so you should sow them so that they are surrounded by friends (but not sitting on top of each other!).

Sow seeds thinly is quite the opposite – some seeds need space and don't want to sit next to their friends. When you sow thinly you plant your seeds making sure none of them are touching.

Thinning seedlings: once your seedlings (young plants) start to grow, they will overcrowd each other and won't have enough room to grow healthy and tall. At this point you need to take out every other seedling so that the ones that remain have enough space. You often have to do this more than once as the seedlings make the most of their new space and grow fast. Each time a seedling's leaves start touching its neighbours, you need to thin them again.

A note on foraging safety:
Some plants taste delicious, some plants are healing and some plants will make you very, very sick if you eat them – so sick you might end up in hospital. When you are out foraging, whether it is in your garden, in a park or out on a walk, always check with your adult before you touch or pick anything, and certainly before a plant gets to your mouth. You may have to take your leaf or flower home and, with your adult, check it in a few reference books. It is much better to wait and make sure you have the right plant than to end up sick.

A note for your adult:
Don't assume you have the right plant. If you think it looks correct but aren't quite sure, don't experiment. Go home and cross reference it. If a leaf or flower smells odd when you crush it then don't taste it – check it in a reference book or speak to an expert.

Gardening Equipment

You will need a few basic pieces of equipment for some of the activities in this book. Many of these items can be created from things you already have in your recycling bin, such as old takeaway trays, milk cartons and yoghurt pots.

Plant Pots

in different sizes – 9 cm, 15 cm, 30 cm and 40 cm in diameter at the top of the pot (see p.46 to make your own)

Seed Trays

(recycled takeaway trays are ideal)

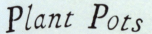

Watering Can

(see p.61 to make your own)

Peat-free Compost

(this is the best compost to choose for the environment)

Plant Labels

(see p.33 to make your own)

Secateurs

(if your adult doesn't have these then a pair of strong scissors will often do)

Hoe

(this is only needed for one or two of the outdoor growing activities)

Hand Trowel

(if your adult doesn't have a trowel you can use a wooden spoon from the kitchen)

Rake

(this is only needed for a few of the outdoor growing activities)

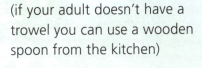

Seed Starting Guide for Growing Plants

You can tell what a seed needs by its size. Tiny seeds will need light to germinate and must be sown on top of the soil. Big seeds, such as peas, broad beans, runner beans, sunflower, marigold and nasturtiums don't need to see the sun, so they should be buried just under the surface of the soil.

How to Sow Seeds

You will need:
- A pot or recycled takeaway tray (make sure there are holes in the bottom) or a bit of the garden or allotment with no weeds
- Compost
- Watering can (see p.61 to make your own)
- Hand rake or trowel
- Seeds!
- A plant label (see p.33 to make your own)

1 You can either sow seeds outside or in your pot or tray. If you're sowing in the ground, make sure you've pulled up all the weeds and that the soil is nice and fluffy. You can use a hand rake or trowel to do this.

2 If you are sowing in a pot or a tray, fill this right up to the top with compost and then gently tap the pot or tray up and down on a hard surface to settle the compost. Seeds like to start life in a nice smooth, well-made bed.

3 Carefully open up the seed packet and take out a small handful of seeds. If your seeds are small scatter them over the compost. If your seeds are bigger then you'll need to cover them with compost.

One way of doing this is using the plant label to draw a line in the compost or, if you are sowing in the ground, you could use a trowel or hoe. Then scatter the seeds down the line. Try and scatter them so they don't fall all on top of one another. No one likes their sibling sitting on their head!

Growing

4 Next, water the seedlings in. If you are outside this can be done with a watering can, but if you are sowing in a tray or pot there are two ways of doing this:

a) You can use a small watering can with a rose on it or your homemade one.

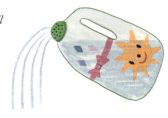

b) You can sit the pot or tray in some water (the washing-up bowl is perfect for this) and the compost will soak up all the water it needs. When the surface of the compost is wet then you can take the pot or tray out. This is a really good trick for tiny seeds that might get moved and sloshed about from water from a can.

5 Now you need to label the seedlings so you don't forget what you're growing. It's also a good idea to write on the date so you know how long it took them to germinate. If they don't come up after a couple of weeks then it usually means they have rotted off.

6 You need to keep your seeds moist, but don't water again utill the seedlings pop up. They need a little greenhouse to keep them moist. This could be a CLEAR plastic bag, yoghurt pot or takeaway tray.

Most seeds need warmth to get going – a sunny kitchen windowsill is perfect.

Once your seedlings are up, you can take off the clear plastic lid or bag and let them have some fresh air.

Very bright sunlight is often too much for tiny seedlings. If the sun is too bright on your windowsill ask an adult to help you find a window ledge with bright but indirect light.

Did you know that seedlings love to be stroked?

Every few days very gently stroke your seedlings. This stimulates them to grow more roots. They also love being talked to! When you talk to a plant you breathe out carbon dioxide, which is what they breathe in to grow. So, every time you sing or talk to your seedlings you are giving them more energy to grow with.

Grow Your Own Tomato Plant

Growing Seedlings

Plant a slice of tomato and watch a forest appear!

1 Take your ripe tomato and cut a slice about 1–2 cm thick. Make sure to get an adult to help you with this.

You will need:
- A large, ripe tomato
- An adult to help slice your tomato
- A 9cm or bigger pot
- Compost
- A clear plastic bag
- A saucer
- A watering can
- A sunny windowsill

2 Fill ¾ of your pot with compost, then carefully place your slice of tomato on top and cover it with more compost.

3 Next, water in the pot so that the compost is wet and sit it on a saucer on a sunny windowsill. To speed everything up you can cover the pot with a clear plastic bag or a recycled clear plastic container. This will act as the pot's own mini greenhouse. Now you have to wait. If all goes well it will take a week, but if the temperature's a bit cool it might take two.

The tomato slice in its bed of compost will start to rot down and with it all the gooey stuff. When this happens the tomato seeds will wake up. They'll pop up through the compost and you'll see a thick forest of seedlings waving hello.

The next step is to nurture your baby tomato forest into full grown plants!

Planting Seedlings

Growing

The tomato forest may look thick and lush, but if we leave all the baby plants together then they'll never grow big. Each one needs its own pot if you want to grow tasty tomatoes.

You will need:
- Your baby tomato plant
- 9 cm pots
- Compost
- A plant label
- A watering can
- Chopsticks
- Newspaper

1 First, lay out your newspaper over a table (make sure you have plenty because this job is messy).

2 Fill up your 9 cm pots to the top with loose compost and then stick your finger in the middle of each pot and wiggle it about a bit to make a hole. The hole needs to go down to ¾ of the depth of the pot.

3 Carefully tip your tomato forest out onto the newspaper, but make sure the seedlings don't land on their heads – no one likes to fall out of bed this way!

4 Take your chopstick and use it to tease apart the babies: holding the baby leaves (never the stem) very, very gently pull the seedling away from its friends. You might have to gently tease apart the roots too. Try not to tear any.

5 Still holding your seedling by its baby leaves, drop it into the hole in your pot of fresh compost so that the baby leaves sit on the surface of the compost.

6 Carefully tap the pot on the table so that the compost settles around the seedling and give it a good water. Now put your potted seedling back on the windowsill and wait for it to grow some more. Repeat this for each of your other seedlings until they are all in new individual pots.

continued on next page ...

continued from page 13

After a few weeks your seedlings should have two sets of leaves – their adult leaves and their baby leaves. Can you tell them apart yet? Adult leaves often have many edges while baby leaves are simple and usually rounder. At first baby leaves are larger than the adult ones, but soon it's the other way around.

The baby leaves are like your baby teeth, they are designed to fall off! When you're handling a seedling you always want to hold them by their baby leaves because it doesn't matter so much if they are damaged a bit.

Potting On

When your feet grow you need a new pair of shoes, and when a seedling grows it needs a new pot. The seedling will let you know this because its roots will start poking out of the bottom of the pot. When you see white roots appear in the drainage holes, it's time to pot on to a bigger sized pot.

1. Fill the bottom ¼ of your pots with compost.

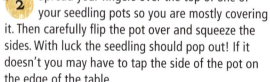

2. Spread your fingers over the top of one of your seedling pots so you are mostly covering it. Then carefully flip the pot over and squeeze the sides. With luck the seedling should pop out! If it doesn't you may have to tap the side of the pot on the edge of the table.

You need to be as gentle as possible so as not to shock the seedling. This is one task you might need to ask an adult to help you with.

You will need:

- Newspaper (or something to cover the table)
- Compost
- Bigger pots (some 15 cm and some 40 cm wide x 40 cm deep)

Growing

There are over 10,000 different varieties of tomato in red, pink, yellow, orange, black, purple, green and even white. Some have stripes, some have bulges, some are huge and some are very small.

Green sausage

There's one variety of tomato called green sausage which is long, pointed and green and yellow striped, and another variety called moneymaker because it's said it produces so many tomatoes that the grower can get rich selling them.

The heaviest tomato was grown in the US by a guy named Dan and it weighed 3.951 kg – that's about the same weight as a cat. Think how much tomato soup you would get out of that!

3 Now place the seedling and as much of the compost as possible into the new 15 cm pot and top it up with more compost so that it's full to the brim.

4 When your plant has grown out of this pot it can be potted up in its final home. For a tomato to grow big and happy, it needs lots of roots and a big pot for these to have space. Time for your 40 cm x 40 cm pot!

5 Pot in the big pot exactly the same way you did the smaller pots in steps 2 and 3, and bury as much of the stem as you can, right the way up to the first set of leaves.

By now your tomato plant will be way too big for the kitchen windowsill, so it's time for it to live outside. A tomato needs to be somewhere very warm to be truly happy.

Foraging for Leaves that Taste Wild

Early humans didn't eat things like carrots, broccoli or sweetcorn. Instead they ate wild plants – the kinds of things that we think of as weeds and wildflowers.

So, let's go find some ancient wild foods and see how they taste! You will need your adult for this activity.

GOLDEN RULES FOR FORAGING:

1 Never eat anything that you are not sure of. Always ask an adult first to be certain you've got the right plant.

2 Don't pick anything next to a road - the pollution from cars is not good for you. You also shouldn't eat anything with dog pee on it. It tastes really, really horrible! Dogs tend to pee on the edge of longer grasses, so pick your leaves a little further in.

3 Don't uproot any wild plant. Only pick the leaves that you need.

4 Don't pick too much: all the bees, butterflies, mice, rabbits, squirrels, voles, shrews, spiders, millipedes and birds rely on wild plants for their food and their homes. We need to make sure we always leave enough for all the others.

Foraging

Garlic Mustard

Garlic mustard likes growing in hedges or on grassy banks. It has bright green heart-shaped leaves and tiny white flowers which are equally delicious.

See if you can spot any tiny orange eggs on the leaves. Garlic mustard is a very important food plant for orange-tip butterflies.

When you and your adult have found the right plant, pick a leaf and crush it in your hands. It should smell of garlic!

When you first put it in your mouth it will taste very hot and spicy like mustard, but then as you keep on chewing it will start to taste like garlic.

Sheep's Sorrel

Sheep's sorrel is always found growing in damp, grassy areas, often where there are sheep grazing. It's never found growing in the shade or away from grass.

When you have the right plant, pick a few leaves and pop them in your mouth. They are very tart, but delicious. They're great to eat when you're feeling a bit thirsty on a long, hot walk.

It has arrow-shaped small leaves about 3 cm long and a tall flower stem with yellow-green or pinkish flowers.

Sheep's sorrel tastes like citrusy sherbet – it zings in the mouth and has a sharp lemon flavour.

17

FLOWERS

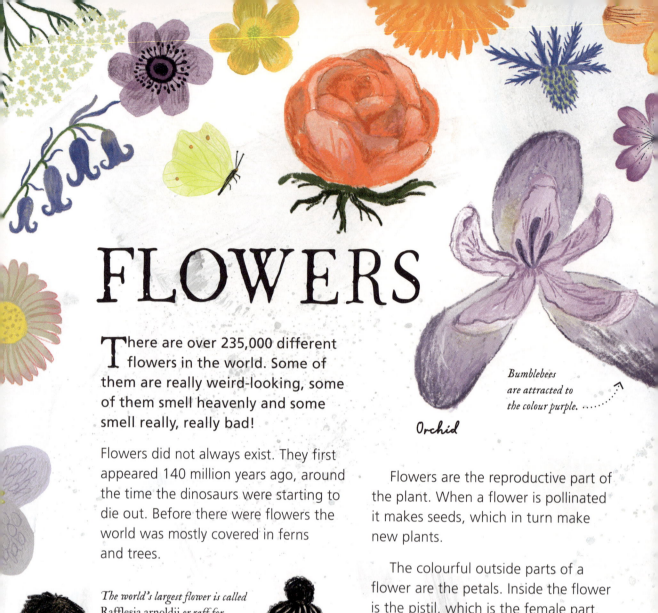

Bumblebees are attracted to the colour purple.

Orchid

There are over 235,000 different flowers in the world. Some of them are really weird-looking, some of them smell heavenly and some smell really, really bad!

Flowers did not always exist. They first appeared 140 million years ago, around the time the dinosaurs were starting to die out. Before there were flowers the world was mostly covered in ferns and trees.

The world's largest flower is called Rafflesia arnoldii or raff for short and can grow up to 1 metre wide. It is also very, very smelly!

Flowers are the reproductive part of the plant. When a flower is pollinated it makes seeds, which in turn make new plants.

The colourful outside parts of a flower are the petals. Inside the flower is the pistil, which is the female part. It looks a bit like a vase with a long neck. The top of the vase is called a stigma – this is sticky and catches the pollen. The bottom part of the vase is the ovary and once pollinated will turn into seeds.

The male part of the flower is called the stamen and on top of that sits the pollen. The pollen is usually round and bright yellow or orange, though in some plants it can be bright purple.

Pollinators such as bees, flies, wasps, beetles, birds and small animals, usually bats, come to gather the pollen from the flowers. Pollen is full of protein: it's really nutritious but quite bitter tasting, so pollinators often mix it with nectar to make it taste nice. Like pouring sugar on your cornflakes!

Some flowers are delicious and some flowers are very, very poisonous. Just a mouthful of a Datura would kill you! In the past it was known as the devil's snare.

Plants need friends with wings!

When a pollinator visits a flower, it collects some of the pollen for itself, but some of the pollen gets stuck, usually on its coat. When the pollinator visits another flower to get more food, the pollen from the previous flower drops into the new flower and gets stuck on that sticky stigma. This fertilises the eggs inside the ovary and the eggs turn into seeds.

So every time a bee or a butterfly visits a plant, it helps it to make seeds, which in turn make new plants.

The reward for doing all this hard work is the pollen and the nectar.

Many flowers are colourful to attract pollinators, but some plants use the wind instead of animals. Wind-pollinated flowers tend to be dull in colour, have no nectar and almost no smell. All grasses are wind-pollinated.

The bird of paradise is a beautiful tropical flower that looks like a colourful bird.

Bird of paradise

The smallest flowering plant in the world is called Wolffia augusta. *It is a tiny water plant and is just 0.6mm long (it could fit inside the letter O on this page).*

Broccoli is actually a flower.

Broccoli

Make a Home for Minibeasts

Ladybirds love to hide in the cracks and crevices of trees...
Spiders hunker down in holes...
Beetles bury themselves in banks...

Once upon a time our world was wild and there were so many nooks and crannies for insects and minibeasts to make their homes in.

But now the concrete of our pavements and paths is too hard to offer comfy holes for tiny creatures to rest, our buildings are too smooth and shiny and don't have enough cracks for insects to live in, and our fields and farms are too clean and cleared for there to be minibeast-friendly hollows.

But in your garden, your park and on your walk to school, you can find thousands of bits and pieces that can be made into a home for minibeasts.

Here are some things you could collect to make a home for minibeasts:

- Dry plant stems from the garden or park
- Hollow shoots from the allotment
- Old hollow bamboo canes
- Twigs from the wood or park
- Tufts of dry moss
- A handful of old straw
- An old terracotta pot or brick with some holes in it
- Pine cones, dry autumn leaves and wood chippings

There are lots of different ways to make a home for minibeasts. Here's just a few ideas to get you started:

Tie the twigs, stems and canes into bundles or wrap them up into rounds, or you could stick them in old cardboard tubes.

Using an old terracotta pot – it doesn't matter if it's cracked but be careful of sharp edges – fill it with the moss or dried leaves, straw or wood chippings you collected and lie it on its side. You can do the same with bricks with holes in.

You can also fill an old wooden box with a layer of straw or leaves and put pine cones on top.

Even just a pile of big pebbles, a small stack of rocks or a small mound of slate will work. As long as there are hidey-holes and tiny cracks, the minibeasts will move in.

Some minibeasts like to spend the winter dry and snug and others like it damp and cool, so there's no one perfect spot for your minibeast home. Just tuck it somewhere away from the rain. Maybe that's under the eaves of a shed roof or window ledge or simply beneath an evergreen bush or a hedge or fence.

Grow Your Own Lunch

Pea shoots are baby pea plants. They taste just like peas and you eat the whole shoot top.

You can grow pea shoots all year round. In the summer you can grow them outside and in the winter you can grow them on a windowsill.

Pea shoots are very good in sandwiches, salads, in tacos, on top of burgers, with fish fingers or just nibbled on their own.

1 Fill your container ¾ full with compost and place the pea seeds on top. You can cram the peas in so they are very close together.

2 Now cover them up with a bit more compost and give them a really good water. If you are growing your peas inside, put your pot on a windowsill and make sure you've got a saucer underneath it to catch the water.

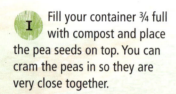

3 Pea shoots are super speedy – they should start to appear in three or four days. When they are 5–10 cm tall, ask an adult to help you cut your first batch with a pair of scissors. How do they taste?

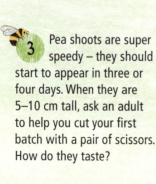

Growing

You will need:
- A pot or other container with drainage holes
- Pea seeds
- Small bag of compost
- Scissors

You can use any pea seeds including dried peas from the supermarket. My favourite brand is Leo Peas because I like the lion on the front of the package. And you don't need a fancy pot, any container will do.

The flowers are just as delicious as the shoots and look lovely sprinkled over your plate.

4 After you've harvested your first pea shoots, give the pot another very good water to speed along the next flush of leaves. If the weather is hot you might need to water your pot every day. You can usually get at least three harvests of peas before the pea plants start to grow very tough and a little bit bitter and don't taste so nice.

5 After a while, when the pea shoots become too tough, if you've got space, replant them outside. Divide up the pot in four sections and give each section a new place to grow. They will flower very quickly as they will be quite exhausted with all the picking you've been doing.

Make Your Own Flower Perfume

Star jasmine

Scent is a plant's way of advertising itself to pollinators and the further away the scent carries on the breeze the more insects the plant can attract to pollinate the flowers and produce seed.

Some plants don't smell at all and that's because they have no nectaries, which are glands where the scent is produced. If you are a grass or sweetcorn or a pine tree, you use the wind to carry your pollen to fertilise the eggs, and so you don't need pollinators to do the work. It would be a waste of energy to create smell, so these plants don't bother.

The smells are sending signals like 'delicious nectar here' or 'come taste my sweet stuff'.

You will need:

- An adult
- A clear jar to keep the perfume in
- A saucepan
- A wooden spoon
- At least a cup's worth of flowers (roses, honeysuckle, star jasmine and lavender are all great)
- Food colouring
- 2 cups of water
- Funnel

1 Once you have all your flowers ready, in a saucepan measure out two cups of water and, asking your adult to help you, bring this to the boil.

2 Add your petals and bring the water down to a simmer. Put a lid on the saucepan so as not to lose any perfume.

Honeysuckle

Activity

Stop and Smell the Roses!

Why don't you have a walk around the garden or local park and smell all the flowers you can find? Remember to check inside the flower first before you shove your nose in – otherwise you might meet a bee!

Flowers tend to smell best first thing in the morning and again in the evening. In the middle of the day, especially if it is very hot, the perfume would be burnt off by the hot sun so the plant doesn't bother producing any.

You could take a notebook with you and draw the flowers you find that have the most interesting smells. Make sure to write down where you found them and what they smell like so you can get to know each plant's particular scent.

For the perfume-making activity you will need to collect some flowers that smell good. Remember to ask permission from your adult before you pick someone else's flowers. You want to pick the whole flower, not just the petals.

3 After two hours turn the hob off. Now you need to wait for the water to cool right the way down. While this is happening, you could decorate your perfume jar.

4 Once the water is cool – ask an adult to check this – you can strain out the last of the perfume from the plant into your perfume jar. Using a wooden spoon, squeeze all the juice out of the flowers and using a funnel pour into your jar. The flowers can now go on the compost heap.

5 The remaining liquid is your perfume. It may be a bit of a funny colour so you could add a drop or two of food colouring to it to make it look better.

Your perfume should keep for about a month in the fridge. If you've made your perfume out of lavender, you could add the whole thing to your bedtime bath.

Grow an Air Plant

Air plants are found in the rainforests, mountains and deserts of the Americas, where they grow in the strangest way possible, high up in the air. They grow on telephone wires, tree branches, bark and rocks, and anything else they can cling onto. And they do all this without any soil, which means they don't need to have lots of roots.

You can buy air plants cheaply online or from a garden centre. There are many different types and you can have quite the collection in a very small space.

1 Air plants want to grow somewhere very humid – that means somewhere with lots of moisture in the air. In your home there are two places that regularly get wet: your bathroom and by the kitchen sink.

2 Air plants don't need very bright conditions because they grow in the canopy of trees, so as long as someone takes a shower or bath regularly, your air plants will be very happy. You can hang them from the ceiling on string or mount them on bark to hang on the wall. Or you can grow them near the kitchen sink.

Growing

When you look at an air plant you often don't see any roots, particularly when they are babies. They do grow a few, which are used to cling on to things, but these roots don't take up water or food.

So how does an air plant live if it doesn't have roots to feed it?

Well, it has special hairy cells on its leaves that allow it to trap moisture in the air. Many air plants grow high up in cloud forests of tropical mountains where there is mist all day long for them to drink.

They may get lots of water, but food is in short supply, which is why these plants grow very slowly.

3 Once a week in the summer, and once a month in the winter, you'll need to give your air plants a good drink. This is the fun bit:

You can also mist your air plants – you can do this as often as you like. If you want to be really kind, once in a while you can find some wet moss outside and squeeze it over your air plant. This will give it a feed and if you do this regularly you may find ...

Fill the sink with water and dunk the plants in for 10 seconds. You can watch them turn from dull grey-green to bright green as all those special hairy cells get woken up and take a drink.

Once you take them out, give them a really good shake to make sure there's no water trapped in the centre as that will rot them off.

... if you are very, very lucky, because it's quite a rare event, that one day your plant might change colour altogether! It may go from grey-green to bright pink or orange or purple. The colour change will start in the middle of the plant until the whole thing blushes. This is the plant's way of signalling to any passing bees or wasps that it is about to flower.

27

Grow a New Succulent from Leaves

Every living thing on Earth is made up of cells – you, me, the street cat, the songbirds, the worms, the amoeba in the soil, the jellyfish and whales in the sea. Cells make up everything: they are the building blocks of life.

Plant cells are amazing because one day they might be a root, but very quickly if that's not working out for them, they can become a stem or a shoot. This allows the plant to make new plants in strange and funny ways, which is how you can turn a leaf into a new plant or get a root to grow into a shoot.

This is called vegetative propagation – two very long words that describe how plants will do anything to find new ground to grow in. They may not have feet to run around the world, but they have many other ways to get around.

One of the amazing things about succulent leaves is that they will all grow roots if given the chance. Succulents have very special leaves full of cells that know how to quickly turn from being a leaf into being a root!

To see how this is done you need to go out and find a succulent. Perhaps your grown-up, a friend or a teacher has one. All you need is a few leaves from their succulent.

You will need:

- An old takeaway tray from your recycling box
- Compost
- A saucer
- Grit or perlite

1 You want to collect a few leaves so gently shake the succulent or tug at one of the bottom leaves that looks healthy. It's best to ask the plant's owner if you can do this first!

2 Next you have to wait for the leaves to callous over (dry and harden) on the end that came away from the stem. This can be done in any saucer or tray. It will take about five days.

Growing

3 Then fill your takeaway tray with compost and some grit or perlite if possible (ask your adult if they have this) as this will help keep the soil from getting too damp and heavy.

4 Don't water it or else it will rot off. Place the tray somewhere bright, but out of direct sunlight. Once a week mist the plants to encourage roots.

5 After a week you should see tiny little roots, though it may take more than a week so be patient!

6 After a while, you'll start to see tiny baby leaves appear – your new plant is growing!

7 After several months you'll have a lot of baby succulents that can be potted up into their own individual pots.

Some succulents that are very easy to propagate are echeverias, kalanchoes, jade plants, burro's tail and jelly bean plants.

Grow Your Own Avocado Tree

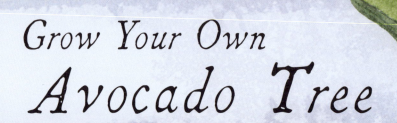

Us humans love avocados – we've been eating them for over 10,000 years. They come from the Tehuacán Valley, in Mexico.

The avocado pip in the centre is a giant seed. It's thought that when the avocado first evolved, back when woolly mammoth and other very large beasts roamed the Earth, the fleshy fruit was swallowed whole by large animals and then the pip was pooped out in their dung, ready to sprout.

Unfortunately for the avocado, but fortunately for us, today there aren't any animals big enough to swallow the fruit whole and poo out the pip. Which is where you come in: now if we want new avocado plants, we need to sprout the pip in water rather than poo!

You will need:

- An avocado pip
- A plastic bottle (if using the plastic bottle method)
- Toothpicks and a jam jar or glass (if using the toothpick method)
- An adult
- Scissors
- A deep pot (15 cm pot should do)
- Compost

The Plastic Bottle Method

1. First, wash and dry your avocado pip.

2. Then, with an adult, cut the top ¼ of a plastic bottle off, just below the neck. This will be where your pip is going to sit. Turn the cut-off bottle top upside down and carefully fit it into the bottom of the plastic bottle, so the neck is now inside the bottle.

If you don't have a plastic bottle you could try...

The Toothpick Method

Growing

Stick three or four toothpicks evenly spaced out into the side of the avocado pip.

Fill a drinking glass or jam jar with water and balance your pip on the top of the glass or jar (making sure the wide bottom side of the pip is sitting in the water). Then put your glass or jam jar on a sunny windowsill and wait.

3 Now fill it up with tap water so that the water reaches inside the neck.

4 Next you need to place your avocado pip inside the upturned bottle neck. The roots will appear from the wide bottom side of the pip, so that bit has to sit in the neck with its bum in the water.

5 Now you can put your avocado on a warm, sunny windowsill and wait very patiently – avocados can take months to germinate, but once they do they move very fast!

You may have to top up your growing system because if your pip doesn't have a wet bum it won't sprout!

continued on next page ...

How to Grow your Sprouted Avocado Pip into a Tree

1. When your pip sprouts, it will have between one to three leaves on it. Once it is at least 10 cm tall you can pot it up into soil. Choose a pot that is deep enough to take its roots without squishing them and fill the pot with fresh compost.

2. The soil is going to seem very dry for your pip after living in a water bottle, so you need to keep watering it regularly. If the edges of the leaves go brown and crispy that's a sign the plant needs more water.

3. When your avocado plant is 20–30 cm high, and has four or more leaves, you need to snip the top off. Cut just above one of the lower leaves so that you remove the top part. This will make the plant branch out into a much more attractive shape. Otherwise you will end up with a very tall and lanky tree.

Your avocado plant will grow as big as you let it. Avocado plants can't grow outside in cold climates, but they love it indoors and like to be warm. If you want a huge tree, then every time you see roots poking out of the bottom of the container it's time to replant it in a bigger pot.

The bigger the pot, the bigger it will grow!

Make Your Own Plant Labels

Activity

Plants have many different names.

They have a Latin name, such as *Calendula officinalis*. *Calendula* is like their surname and *officinalis* is their first name. They may have many common names as well. These are like nicknames. *Calendula officinalis* is also known as pot marigold or sometimes common marigold.

And then there's the names you give your own plants. I have a houseplant called Fred that's been with me for over 20 years. We've moved everywhere together!

It's so easy to forget what plants you've sown, so rather than getting all your seedlings mixed up you can use plant labels.

As well as the name you can also put other useful information on the label, like:

The date you sowed the seeds. This way if your seedlings don't wake up a couple of weeks after you sowed them, you can check the date and see if it's a case of waiting a bit longer or starting again.

Your name so that your seedlings don't get mixed up with your brother's/sister's/cat's/dad's seedlings.

Some things that you can recycle to make labels:

Nice flat pebbles work well as labels. You can either paint on them or write on them with a permanent marker pen. These are great in the garden for things that you sow lots of, such as basil, lettuce, beetroot, thyme …

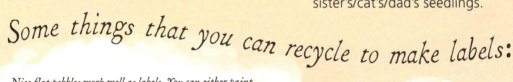

You can cut labels out of yoghurt pots. With an adult's help, slice off the bottom and then cut the sides into strips or triangles. You'll need to write on them with a permanent marker pen.

Lollipop sticks make excellent labels.

If you live near a beach you could collect large seashells. You can write inside them!

SEEDS

Seeds come in every shape and size you can imagine. They are the part of the plant that can grow into a new plant. Seeds are alive and they carry all they need to start off a new life. They are packed with food that helps the new plant grow.

A seed is asleep, until it germinates, when it wakes up and begins to grow into a little plant called a seedling. When you sow a seed, you are giving it all it needs to wake up – which is water, air and light.

The smallest seeds in the world are made by orchids. They are tiny, smaller than a speck of dust. They are so small that they can float away, often on the wind, sometimes on water. They can float on the wind for over 1000 miles.

Water

The first thing a seed needs is water, so that it can swell up and burst open its seed coat. Once it's taken its coat off it can grow its roots. This allows the seed to anchor itself into its new home and makes sure it's upright.

Orchid

Avocado

When a squirting cucumber is ripe, its fruit falls off and at the same time spits all its seeds out in a long stream of slime. It can spit its seed out to 6 m away!

SUPER SEEDERS
The squirting cucumber

HOW TO GROW YOUR SEEDS

Air

The next thing the seed needs is air, which contains oxygen. The oxygen starts off all sorts of processes inside the seed, releasing food so the seedling can have its first breakfast. If your seeds are too wet, they won't get enough oxygen and this is often why they don't wake up.

Light

The final thing the seed needs is light. Once the seeds have had a good drink, taken off their coat and had their first meal, they send out their baby leaves to get some sun. Light is needed so the seedlings can make their own food every day.

The largest seed in the world is from a palm tree called a coco de mer, which means 'coconut of the sea'. It can reach up to 30 cm long and weigh up to 18 kg. It looks just like a baboon's bottom.

GARDEN WEEKLY

coco de mer

How Plants Take Up Water

Plants take up water through their roots and it travels all the way up the plant right to the very top leaves. Just think of how far water has to travel to get to the top of a tall tree!

Water moves through a plant pretty fast. It travels up tall plants at about the same speed as a lift in a tall building does.

You can do a very simple experiment to see how water travels, and you can even see which parts of the plant it travels through, using some water with food colouring in.

How this experiment works

Plants take up water from their roots and it is pulled up through the stem right the way to the very top of the leaves through special cells called xylem tubes.

These tubes are made up of overlapping long, hollow cells. As these cells grow, they stretch out, die and leave behind hollow cavities that interconnect to make one long hollow tube.

It is a bit like connecting lots of drinking straws together from the tip of the root right the way to the top of the plant. Imagine how many drinking straws you would need for a tree!

You will need:
- Chinese cabbage or celery stalks with their leaves still attached
- Brightly coloured food colouring
- A few glasses and water at room temperature
- A magnifying glass

1 If you are using Chinese cabbage then just peel the leaves off the plant carefully. This experiment works best if the leaves are roughly the same height and size. The bigger the leaf the longer the experiment will take.

2 our adult to carefully cut 1–2 cm off the bottom of the celery stem or Chinese cabbage leaf using a sharp knife.

Carnation

Experiment

3 Now half fill your glasses with water and add enough food colouring to dye the water a deep colour. 10 drops is usually enough.

4 Place your celery stalks or Chinese cabbage in the water.

5 Depending on how warm the room is, the plants will start taking up the dye after about an hour, but the best results will be seen the next day.

6 Once you've allowed the plants enough time to take up the dye, slice your celery stem or cabbage leaf in half. You should see lots of coloured dots in the stem. These are the cells in the xylem tubes!

You can see them because the food colouring has changed the colour of the water and now you can see where the water is travelling.

7 With a magnifying glass look closely at the stems and leaves and you can trace the xylem all the way up the plant.

Further Experiments

You can also do this experiment with white carnations and chrysanthemums. If you are super careful you can split the stem of the flower in half, leaving the flower intact, and put each half in different coloured water – you'll get half a flower in one colour and half in another. You can do the same trick with the celery and Chinese cabbage.

Edible Flowers

Did you know that you can EAT flowers? That's right, they're not just the pretty parts of a plant that attract insects but can be a tasty addition to your dinner too.

Some flowers taste delicious, some flowers taste of very little, some are super bitter and some are super dangerous and would kill you with just one mouthful! So it's very important that you don't just go around eating any flower that you come upon.

Here are some flowers that are safe to eat, but always check with your adult before eating any to make sure you've identified the right flowers:

Nasturtiums

Nasturtiums are very spicy. I can only eat about three in a row.

Violets

Violets taste like sweet perfume to me. Sweet violets and dog violets are found growing wild at the edge of woodlands, grassy paths and in dappled shade.

Basil flowers

Basil flowers are sweet and perfumed, and you can eat the whole flower head.

Rocket

Rocket is sweet and peppery – it's delicious in salads.

Dandelions

Dandelions are a little bit bitter on their own, but when you cook them in pancake batter they taste wonderful.

Activity

Picking Your Edible Flowers

Warning!
You should only eat flowers that you, or someone you know, have grown because that way you will be sure there are no nasty chemicals on them.

Chive flowers

Chive flowers taste like sweet onions and chive plants are very easy to grow.

Courgette flowers

Courgette flowers are delicious chopped up in pasta sauces.

Pot marigold

Pot marigolds are a vibrant orange colour. They are great on salads and soups. They look pretty, but they don't taste particularly interesting.

There are several things that like to live in flowers that aren't so tasty to eat, so watch out for these when you're picking flowers:

Bees visit flowers for pollen and nectar, but sometimes if it's too dark to get home, they sleep in flowers, so it's always wise to make sure there's not a bee in there before you pick.

Flower beetles are tiny shiny green-black beetles that eat pollen and sometimes there can be quite a few in one flower. The easiest way to get them to move is to blow hard on the flower after you've picked it and then give it a good shake.

Earwigs also love to eat pollen, particularly in the autumn, so sometimes you have to ask them to leave too. Again, just shake the flower and they should drop out.

Do you know how you can tell a female earwig from a male earwig? Well, female earwigs have pointy pincers on their bums, whereas male earwigs have very curved pincers.

39

Nasturtiums

Grow Your Own Edible Flowers

Marigolds and nasturtiums are very easy to grow from seed. There are two different types of marigold: French marigold and pot marigold. You want to grow pot marigold, their Latin name is *Calendula officinalis* (the *officinalis* bit means it is a plant used in traditional herbal medicine). Pot marigold flowers are anti-microbial, which means they fight things like colds, sore throats and infections.

Nasturtiums, *Tropaeolum majus*, come all the way from the Andes in South America, but they love it here and grow very wild very quickly, so you don't need to sow too many seeds.

There are many different colours of both nasturtiums and marigolds. If you want to dye your food orange with pot marigolds (see the recipe on p.43) then choose the seeds that give the most orange petals!

1. If you're planting your seeds outside then you need to sow them in spring, when all the cold weather and frosts have passed. Usually this is at the end of April.

2. The soil needs to be free of weeds and a bit fluffy. Use a hand trowel or a little rake to soften the soil.

You will need:

- Pot marigold seeds OR nasturtium seeds
- A large pot and soil (if you're growing your seeds indoors, otherwise choose a sunny spot in the garden)
- A watering can
- A hand trowel
- A label

Tip: To tell if the soil is warm enough you can wiggle your fingers into the soil and see how long you can leave them there. If you have to take them out immediately then it's still too cold!

Growing

3 If you are using a pot, it needs to be large enough to allow the plant enough space. In a pot that is 30 cm wide, I plant just two seeds! Fill your pot almost to the top with soil.

4 Then, either in the ground or in your pot, using your fingers, poke a hole up to your knuckle, pop two seeds in and cover the hole over with some loose soil.

5 If you want to plant a number of seeds outside then you need to make sure each seed is 30 cm apart, which is about four of your handspans.

6 Give the ground or the soil in your pot a water and wait for the seedlings to pop up.

7 Once the seedlings are up remove the smaller one by carefully pulling it out. This lets the other, bigger seedling grow even bigger. If you didn't pull one out, both seedlings would suffer.

Pot marigold

Marigold tea

Dried marigold petals make a lovely tea that helps to keep colds at bay, but it is a little bitter so I always add some honey.

41

Edible Flower Recipes:

Dandelion Pancakes

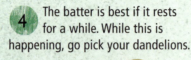

You will need:
- 100 g plain flour
- 1 large egg
- 300 ml milk (or milk substitute)
- A knob of butter or coconut oil
- Dandelion flowers
- Maple, date or golden syrup

1 First, place the flour in a large bowl and make a well in the centre. Crack the egg into a glass and pour this into the well.

2 Beat the egg with a whisk, gradually drawing the flour into the mix.

3 When the egg is all beaten, slowly pour in the milk, whisking all the time, until you have a smooth batter.

4 The batter is best if it rests for a while. While this is happening, go pick your dandelions.

You want open flowers that are as big as possible. If you don't have any at home, go with your grown-up to the park. The best dandelions tend to be at the edges of open grassy spots. The stalk of a dandelion flower tastes very bitter, so you don't want any stalk on the flowers.

5 When you get back to the kitchen, dust off the flowers, but don't wash them or they'll end up like soggy tissues!

6 Ask your adult to melt some butter in a hot frying pan while you dip the flowers into the batter. You can then place them upside down on a clean plate, whilst you wait for the frying pan to heat up.

7 Once the pan is hot enough your adult can fry your dandelion pancakes for you until they are golden brown.

Now the fun bit: put as many dandelion pancakes as you want on a plate, drizzle with a little syrup and eat them!

Orange Cheese Sauce

Activity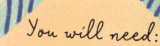

You will need:
- 500 ml milk (or milk substitute)
- 4 tablespoons plain flour
- 50 g butter
- 100 g cheddar cheese
- 2-4 tablespoons finely chopped pot marigold petals

1 Pour 500 ml milk into a large saucepan and add the pot marigold flowers and, with the help of your adult, very gently heat the milk.

2 When the petals are starting to colour the milk, add the flour and the butter.

4 Whisk for another 2 minutes while the sauce bubbles then stir in the cheese until melted. Pour your sauce over your pasta or vegetables.

You could add a few whole petals to decorate the dish at the end if you fancy.

3 Turn up the heat to medium and start to whisk the mixture. Keep whisking fast as the butter melts and the mixture comes to the boil – the flour will disappear and the sauce will begin to thicken.

This cheese sauce can be used on cauliflower or broccoli or just on pasta. You could also pour it over vegetables and add bread crumbs and potato wedges on top and bake it.

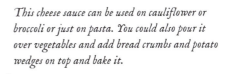

Pot marigold gets its name from the cooking pot – they have long been added to sauces and stews.

LEAVES

Leaves come in all shapes, sizes and textures. Some are as big as an umbrella, some are hairy, some are furry, some are waxy, some have spines, some sting and some smell delicious!

There are even some leaves which contain powerful medicines that can help against pain and others that are full of poison.

When a plant is a baby seedling it has baby leaves. Eventually the plant has to lose these so the adult leaves can grow.

The shape of a leaf often tells you lots about where the plant comes from. Blue or grey leaves are found on plants that live in very bright sunny places – the blue-grey reflects the strong sunlight, a bit like a plant deciding to wear sunglasses. Plump and leathery leaves like that of a cactus or succulent mean that the plant lives in a place with very little water. The leaves are acting like water bottles, storing up water for when the plant is thirsty.

Leaves are the powerhouse of the plant. They are just like solar panels: they take energy from the sun and convert it into food for the plant to grow. While roots take up water, leaves take in carbon dioxide (that's the stuff you breathe out). The leaves mix the water and the carbon dioxide and then use their solar panels to turn this into sugar and oxygen. This is called **photosynthesis**. Plants use the sugars to grow, and you use the oxygen to breathe. It's as if every time you breathe in, a plant breathes out and vice versa.

Did you know that leaves can move? The Venus flytrap shuts its leaves tight to trap flies so it can gobble them up! The prayer plant folds its leaves up every night before it goes to sleep and then in the morning waves them out again to catch the sun's rays.

Venus flytrap

Cactus

A cactus's spines are actually its leaves. The cactus stores all its water in its stem and develops sharp spines to protect this supply from thirsty creatures in the desert that want to steal it!

Leaves come in all sorts of colours: gold, orange, pink, purple, red and, of course, many shades of green. The green colour in leaves is called chlorophyll. It's like a magical paint that can make its own food and energy.

Make Your Own Plant Pot

The wonderful thing about plants is that they don't care one bit what their pot looks like. You can make your pot as fancy as you like, or you can grow a plant in a plastic bag, so long as it drains. Good drainage is the most important thing for a plant pot.

1 Wash out the carton and make sure that it is completely dry. If there's a label on it, remove this.

You will need:
- Milk or juice carton (needs to be at least 10 cm deep)
- An adult
- Knife and scissors (for your adult to use)
- Acrylic paint
- Old newspaper
- Brushes
- Marker pens

2 Draw a line around the top where you want to cut it. You could draw your line into a zigzag shape, or draw ears, but a straight line is also fine. With your adult helping, use scissors to cut above your line and then cut out your shape.

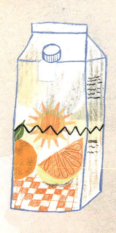

3 Your adult will need to poke some holes in the base for drainage. They will need to use a sharp knife or screwdriver for this.

Activity

I bet you can find lots of things in the recycling that would make an excellent pot. Have a rummage and see if you can find any of these:

Loo roll tubes
Milk or juice carton
Clear plastic container and tray liners
Takeaway trays (aluminium or plastic)
Yoghurt pots
Ice-cream tubs

Loo roll tubes are excellent for starting off seedlings like peas and beans. Once the seedlings are big enough to plant out you can keep them in their tubes and just plant everything in the ground – the cardboard tube will rot away without disturbing the roots. You'll need to collect a lot of loo roll tubes though because this works best if they're all nudged in close together in a tray so they don't dry out.

To create a fancier pot that you can decorate, you can use a milk or juice carton and follow the steps below.

4 Now you're ready to paint your container. Remember to lay out some old newspaper on the surface you're using as this can get a bit messy!

5 You will need two layers of paint – make sure to leave time for the paint to dry between each layer.

6 Once it is fully dry, you can decorate your pot. You could draw a funny face or a pattern or just write your name. Whatever you like!

7 Now all you need to do is fill your pot with compost and plant it up or sow some seeds. And there you have it – your very own homemade plant pot!

How to Make Wildflower Seed Paper

We all use so much paper: doing homework, drawing, writing thank-you letters, sending notes … But have you ever stopped to think how paper is made? Well, now's your chance to find out.

You're going to make recycled paper from paper you've already used. If you're feeling adventurous you can also make your own pink dye for your paper from kitchen peelings (to make your dye so it's ready to add to your paper turn to p.50).

This paper is going to be special because you're going to add wildflower seeds. This way, hidden in your paper is a meadow to help the pollinators. You can use it to write a letter or note to someone and then, once they've read it, they can go outside and plant the paper! Once the paper gets wet from the soil, the little seeds will wake up and start to grow.

This is a very messy and wet activity, so you will need a well-protected work surface and make sure to have plenty of old towels or tea towels handy. It will take two days to complete so be patient!

You will need:

- Mostly white paper from the recycling box – newspaper, old letters, thin, plain cardboard will all work, but nothing too shiny or too coloured
- A big bowl
- Water
- An electric blender and an adult to help you with the blending
- Old towels or tea towels
- A sponge (dishwashing sort is fine)
- A deckle
- A large, deep baking tray (your baking tray needs to be bigger than your deckle)
- Parchment or baking paper
- A mixed pack of wildflower seeds
- Natural dye (optional)

Note:
To make paper you need a deckle, which is a screen used to drain the pulp. You can buy a deckle from an art supply shop or online, but you can also make your own from a wooden picture frame. Ask your adult to do this with you – there are lots of helpful instructional videos online. You can also repurpose a kitchen splatter screen or use an embroidery hoop with plastic mesh.

Deckle

Activity

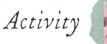

1. Tear the paper into little bits and fill your big bowl with water. Then soak the bits of paper for at least four hours, until the paper is really mushy. Drain off the excess water.

4. Slip the deckle in from the side so that it slides beneath the pulp. Lift the screen up gently, catching the pulp, and let the water drain off. At this point you can use your sponge to make sure the pulp is spread evenly across the deckle.

2. Put the soaked paper in the blender and fill it halfway with water. If you want to add your natural dye to colour your paper, now is the time to do it. Use your dye first and top up with plain water if necessary.

Ask your adult to help you pulse the blender until the mixture is pulped.

5. Sit the deckle on an old towel and using the sponge soak up any excess water.

3. Next, fill your baking tray ¼ full with water and then add the blended paper pulp and mix it up.

6. Now scatter your seeds over the surface of the paper and gently press any larger seeds into the pulp.

continued on next page ...

continued from page 49

Making Your Vegetable Ink Dye

7 Once the surface of the paper begins to dry slightly, you should be able to flip the deckle with the paper onto parchment or baking paper to continue to dry. It will take 24 hours for the paper to dry.

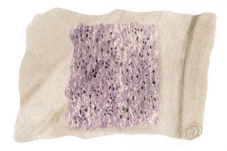

8 If your paper is not very flat then, once it is dry, flatten it with heavy books. Your paper will probably be quite textured and thick (it takes a lot of practice to make very thin paper).

9 When you send your paper meadow to someone remember to include instructions on how to get the seeds to grow.

You can plant the paper straight onto the surface of a pot, or you can rip it up into bits and scatter these over several pots. Then water the paper well and cover with a very thin layer of compost and wait for the seeds to spring!

Red onion skins or beetroot are perfect for making a bright dye.

If you use onion skins then you just need the dry papery outer layer and you want as many as possible to get a deeper dye.

You can use one fresh red beetroot or you can use lots of peelings from many beetroots.

You will need:
- An adult
- A stainless steel saucepan
- Water
- Red onion skins or beetroot (you can also use a mix of both)
- A sieve and muslin cloth to line it

Making your dye will take 2 days.

1 With the help of your adult, chop up your beetroot and/or onion skins into smaller pieces.

Activity

2 Add them to the saucepan and pour over just enough water to cover the pieces.

3 Ask your adult to heat the pan gently with a lid on for 30 minutes. Then they need to take the pan off the heat and let it sit overnight.

4 In the morning, ask your adult to reheat the dye for another 30 minutes. Then turn off the heat and allow the pot to cool for a couple of hours.

5 Strain the dye through a sieve lined with a muslin cloth to catch any of the vegetable pieces.

Ask your adult to repeat this another two times until you get a strong colour.

6 You can add a teaspoon of vinegar to brighten the colour if you wish.

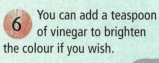
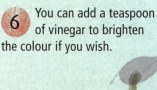

You can use this dye to colour your wildflower seed paper (see step 2 on p.49).

51

Foraging for Roots that Taste Wild

Dandelion Roots

Dandelions are one of my favourite wildflowers – they're so cheerful and tasty (did you try the dandelion pancakes on p.42?).

This time we're going to try eating the roots. In the past people used to boil up and roast the roots to make a sort of coffee substitute. It was used a lot in the Second World War when coffee was hard to get hold of.

The roots can be quite bitter tasting, but if you know the right trick to prepare them you can make them taste delicious.

1 With your adult, first dig up the dandelions with your trowel. You want to find dandelions that are not in flower but have a flower bud at the centre of the plant. It looks like a little round green button in the very centre of the rosette of leaves.

You will need:

- About 10 dandelion plants

  you can forage in the garden or your local park (remember to look at the 'Golden Rules for Foraging' on p.16 first).

- A small trowel
- An adult to help

Flower bud

We also want a bit of the root, about an inch or so long. We're going to eat the heart of the dandelion with a little bit of root attached. This is the sweetest bit of the plant.

Foraging

The word dandelion comes from the French 'dent de lion', meaning lion's teeth.

2 Once you've dug up enough dandelions, take them inside and wash them really well. Then pinch off all the leaves. Rabbits love dandelion leaves, so maybe if you know a rabbit you could give it the leaves as a treat.

3 Now you should be left with a little bit of root, a flower bud in the centre and some leaves around it. Pinch off all the leaves so that you are just left with a little bit of root and the flower bud.

4 Now you need to fry this in some oil and you'll definitely need an adult to help with that. The roots need to be fried for about five minutes, perhaps with a little garlic if you like it, and some salt and pepper.

5 Once they cool down a bit, try them! I like them with spaghetti and cheese.

Herb Bennet Roots

You will need:
- Herb bennet roots
- A small trowel
- An adult to help
- 3 apples
- A sprinkling of sugar
- A knob of butter
- A frying pan

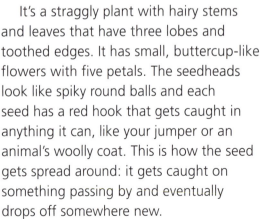

Herb bennet has many names: sometimes it's called wood avens, colewort or St Benedict's herb. Its Latin name is *Geum urbanum*. You find it growing in shady places under hedges, in woods and beneath shrubs in your garden.

It's a straggly plant with hairy stems and leaves that have three lobes and toothed edges. It has small, buttercup-like flowers with five petals. The seedheads look like spiky round balls and each seed has a red hook that gets caught in anything it can, like your jumper or an animal's woolly coat. This is how the seed gets spread around: it gets caught on something passing by and eventually drops off somewhere new.

You're going to use herb bennet roots to add flavour to apple sauce.

1 With your adult, carefully dig up a herb bennet plant and smell the roots. They should smell of cloves.

2 Scrub the roots in the kitchen sink so there's no soil left. Soil doesn't tend to taste great! You can nibble the clean roots to taste them – they will be very spicy and hot.

3 Tie the roots into a knot.

Foraging

4 With the help of your adult, peel and core three apples and then chop them into chunks.

5 Ask your adult to melt a little butter in a pan and then add the apples, the knot of herb bennet roots, a sprinkling of sugar and a splash of water, and cook the apples slowly until they become mush.

6 Once the sauce has cooled, take out the roots as they will now have flavoured the sauce and they are far too chewy to eat.

Try this apple sauce with cream swirled into it as a pudding.

Herb bennet is also known as 'clove-root' because the roots taste somewhere between cloves and cinnamon.

THE NIGHT GARDEN

The garden becomes a very different place at night. While you are all tucked up in bed, a whole new world comes to life ...

Let's meet some of the creatures of the night:

Slugs

Huge fat slugs creep out from their daytime hiding holes and get to work on anything that they decide is delicious ... which may well be your seedlings!

Slugs move about on their stomach and they leave a slimy trail wherever they go. This slime trail has many purposes:

- It helps them glide over bumpy and prickly surfaces.
- It acts as a map for how to get back to bed at the end of the night.
- It tells all the slug's friends what it's been up to – what it's been eating, where it's napped and whether it wants to meet up or not.

Slugs love to eat plants, so gardeners don't like them. Some slugs mow down every new seedling in sight, but the very big black and brown slugs tend to only eat rotting food. They are like the dustbin collectors of the garden.

Leopard slug

Common toad

Bird cherry ermine moth

Ghost moth

Common emerald

Frogs and Toads

Frogs and toads also come out at night, particularly if you have a pond for them to mate in. They like to eat slugs, snails and all manner of other insects.

Have you ever seen a frog eating its tea? I used to look after the frogs at Kew Gardens and spent hours watching them eat. Their long tongue is like a very sticky piece of elastic and they flick it out so fast that bam! The prey gets stuck. Then they recoil their tongue and munch down hard.

Moths

While the beetles are creeping along the ground at night, the air turns to a flurry of flying things as the night moths come out to play.

There are many, many moths – far more moths than butterflies – and lots of them only fly at night. They use the light of the moon to navigate and they drink the nectar of sweet-smelling flowers that bloom in the evening.

If you take a torch and scan it over the garden at night you might catch some moths at play, but if you want to see lots of moths then you need to grow some flowers for them ...

Common frog

Ground Beetles

Ground beetles tend to be black and shiny, sometimes with a violet sheen, and move very fast. If they see you, they'll run away. That's probably because you've disturbed them in the day and they want to go back to bed. They like to sleep under piles of dry leaves, stones and rotting logs. Then as dusk falls, out they come to run about and hunt for food ...

Ground beetles love slug and snail eggs as well as baby slugs and snails. They also eat maggots, wireworms, aphids and caterpillars. This makes them a very good friend to gardeners.

Flowers for Moths

There are three flowering plants you can grow that moths absolutely love: sweet william, wild honeysuckle and common jasmine.

Sweet William

This is a lovely plant that you can grow from seed. You'll love the smell and so will the moths, bees and butterflies. It comes in pink, white and red and grows to about 45 cm high in sunny spots. You want to find varieties that have single flowers, and moths like pink and white flowers best. Double flowers don't have very much nectar in them and so aren't much fun for pollinators. Sow seeds in July to flower the following summer.

The steps below are for growing sweet William (*Dianthus barbatus*) outside but you can also grow it in a seed tray indoors, just follow the seed starting guide on p.10–11. Once your seedlings are a few inches high you will need to move them into 30 cm pots and put them outside.

1. You can sow sweet William seeds straight into the ground but the soil must be free from weeds first.

2. You need to make a line in the soil to sow the seeds into. It needs to be 5 mm deep with 30 cm space between rows. If the soil is dry, water it first.

You will need:
- *Sweet William seeds*
- *A trowel and rake*
- *A plant label*
- *A watering can*

Elephant hawk-moth

Growing

Honeysuckle

Wild Honeysuckle

This is loved by large moths with long tongues. Honeysuckles like to have damp feet and their heads in the sun, so you need to grow them in the shade where they can grow up into a sunny spot. The best one to grow is called *Lonicera periclymenum* 'Graham Thomas'. It will grow to 8 m tall. Plant it just like you would the common jasmine (shown on the next page).

Hummingbird hawk-moth

3 Now, down the line sow the seeds trying to make sure they don't fall on top of one another too much. Cover them up with a little soil.

4 Once the seedlings grow and start to crowd each other out, thin them to 15 cm apart.

5 Once autumn comes you can move the young plants to where you want them to flower. You could leave them in their line or dot them about the garden or put them in 30 cm pots. Each plant needs to be 30 cm apart to grow big.

You must make sure to keep your plants well watered if it doesn't rain and then by next summer you'll have lots of beautiful flowers.

Sweet William

continued on next page ...

continued from page 59

Common Jasmine

This has such a wonderful smell, particularly in the evening. It's a very rampant vine that can grow up to 12 m (that's as tall as a house). Moths love this one and you are bound to see plenty of them visiting it as it flowers from July through to October.

Jasmine moth

1 Using your trowel, dig a large hole and add lots of compost to the hole.

You will need:

- A common jasmine plant: you can get this from a garden centre and grow it outside (if you don't have a garden then why not see if you can grow it in your school garden or at a local allotment?)
- A trowel
- Compost
- A watering can

2 Then, being very careful not to damage the roots, plant your common jasmine in the hole.

3 You will have to water it lots over its first summer, particularly if it doesn't rain. After that it should take care of itself.

Make Your Own Watering Can

Plants can't grow without water. In fact, they will die pretty quickly so one thing that you are definitely going to need is a watering can!

The best watering cans act just like rain: they send soft, fine droplets of water over the plants rather than big gushes of water. On a traditional watering can there's something called a ROSE on the end of the spout to create a gentle rain of water.

If you don't have a watering can you can make one out of a big plastic milk (or juice) carton.

You will need:
- 1 litre (or bigger) plastic milk or juice carton
- A piece of wood you can nail into (NOT the kitchen table!)
- A small nail
- A small hammer
- An adult to help you
- Some marker pens to decorate with

1. Take the lid off the milk carton and place it on your bit of wood so that it sits upright.

2. Ask your adult to hammer a hole into the top of the lid using the nail.

3. Ask them to repeat this until the top of the lid is covered in little holes.

4. Fill the milk carton with water and place the lid back on the top. Now turn it upside down and hey presto – you've got a watering can!

You can decorate your watering can with marker pens to make it your own.

61

Grow Your Own Parsnip Pea-Shooter

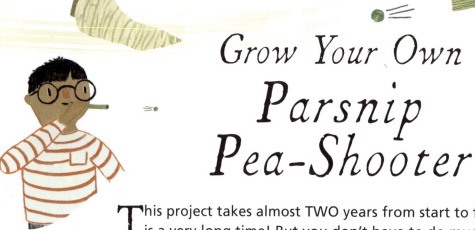

This project takes almost TWO years from start to finish, which is a very long time! But you don't have to do much more than wait and in the meantime the pollinators will be very grateful.

Parsnips are sown in spring and harvested in the autumn and winter. It takes them all summer to get big and fat but if you don't harvest the parsnips and leave them in the ground over winter then the following summer they will flower.

Parsnips have really tall flowers, up to 2.5 m tall (that's bigger than any human), and are covered in bright yellow flowers.

The bees will love you if you let one or two parsnips flower. Their flowers are packed with nectar and pollen and sometimes there are so many bees on the plants that the whole thing sways under the weight of all those pollinators!

How to Sow Parsnips

1. Sow your parsnips on a sunny day in soil that doesn't have any weeds in it. The best time to sow parsnips is between April and the beginning of May.

2. Draw a line in the soil with a hoe. The line needs to be about 1 cm deep, so you just need to draw it gently – it doesn't matter if your line is wiggly.

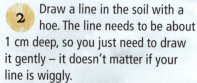

You will need:

- Parsnip seeds
- A sunny spot in the garden or allotment
- An adult to help
- A hoe
- Secateurs or strong scissors
- A label

Growing

3 Parsnips don't like to start off life in very dry soil, so if it hasn't rained recently then water your line.

4 Place your seeds very thinly so they are not touching each other down the line. Then carefully cover them up with some soil.

5 Now write their name on a label and put it at the beginning of the line. You can also put a stick at the end of the line to mark where they are if you like.

6 Parsnips can take over two weeks to germinate so it's important you know where they are to make sure no one plants something else on top of them or, worse still, weeds them out because they didn't know what they were!

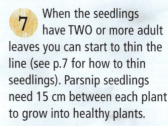

7 When the seedlings have TWO or more adult leaves you can start to thin the line (see p.7 for how to thin seedlings). Parsnip seedlings need 15 cm between each plant to grow into healthy plants.

What to do next...

You only need one or maybe two plants to go to flower next year to make pea-shooters, so when autumn comes around and your parsnips are big and plump, you could eat some of them.

Parsnip soup

After the flowers come the seeds – there will be loads of these! You could save some of the seeds in a brown paper envelope and give them away to a friend who wants to make their own pea-shooter or grow parsnips for their dinner.

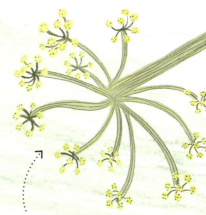

Once the flowers have finished and seeds appear, you'll notice the whole plant goes brown and dry. This is the moment to make your parsnip pea-shooter.

63

Making your Pea-Shooter

1. With your adult, cut down one whole flower's stem and look for the fattest bit. Then with some secateurs cut a section about 10 cm long. You need a straight, clean, hollow section without any leaves. This is your pea-shooter.

2. Place a pea in one end and put your mouth to the other then blow really hard. The pea will fire out!

3. See how far and fast you can shoot your pea, but never aim your pea-shooter at your friends, other humans, your dog or cat, a mouse, squirrel or any other LIVING BEING. No one wants a very fast, hard pea being fired at them.

Warning!

Make sure to always blow out hard rather than suck the end of your shooter so that you don't end up swallowing a pea, which might not be very pleasant.

If you have a lot of stem left you could make a different length shooter and see which one shoots the fastest peas and which one shoots the peas the furthest away.

Stems that Play Tricks

Experiment

How's your tomato plant from p.15 doing? Is it big yet? Do you need to put it into a bigger container so that it can grow as many tomatoes as possible? Well, let's make the stem do its magic trick so that your tomatoes taste as good as possible.

If you look at the stem of your tomato plant, you will see it is covered with hairs. When these hairs touch the earth or are buried in compost, they become the roots. When we repot a tomato plant, we want to make the most of these amazing stems that change into roots!

How to turn a tomato stem into roots

Pinch off the bottom set of leaves using your thumb and fingers. Then when you repot choose a container deep enough that you can cover the stem right the way up to the next set of leaves, burying the stem so that you get many more roots.

Gently fill around the stem with compost and then water the tomato in well. The water will help the stem's hairs to turn into roots.

When the summer is over and all the tomatoes are long gone, you can pull up your tomato plant and check out the buried stem. You'll see there's no longer any stem left and instead there's just a mass of roots! Plants know a lot of magic tricks.

How to Make a Hoverfly Happy

Hoverflies are magical insects; they work so hard in our gardens. Their young eat many pests and the adults do lots of pollination work. In fact, they are amazing pollinators because, unlike bees, they aren't bothered about flying in the rain!

There are many different hoverflies in the world. At the last count there were over 6,000!

It's not always easy to tell a hoverfly from a bee, but if you get up close then look for big round eyes at the front of their head. Also, hoverflies have two wings, whereas bees have four.

Their young look, frankly, revolting. Like something you might want to squish, but you shouldn't. Hoverfly larva eat thousands upon thousands of aphids every year and are truly the friends of gardeners.

larva

One thing that hoverflies universally love to dine on is coriander flowers.

1. Fill your pot with compost and gently press the compost down so that the surface is firm.

2. Scatter the coriander seeds over the compost so that the seeds are 5 cm apart. You will need about five or six seeds. Cover the seeds with a thin layer of compost.

Wait a week or so.

How to Sow Coriander

You can sow coriander from late March through to August outside. Wherever you have some bare, weed-free ground you can scatter the seeds and gently rake them in. For growing inside, follow the steps below:

You will need:

- Coriander seeds (you can buy these from the garden centre or see if there's any in your kitchen cupboard. The seeds in your cupboard will germinate as long as they're not too old).
- Compost
- A 30 cm wide pot
- Watering can

You can eat the leaves of the young coriander plant. Some people think they taste like soap while others think they are delicious! What do you think?

3 Water the seeds in with your watering can.

4 Wait a week or so and your seedlings should be up. It's going to take another month before they flower so keep them in the sun and see how many hoverflies you get.

Harvesting Your Coriander Seeds

Become a Seed Saver!

Once your coriander plant has finished flowering don't pull it up. If you look at where the flower used to be you'll start to see the seed beginning to develop. The seed is round and bright green. This is because it hasn't matured and dried out. The green seed is very delicious – you might want to give some of it to an adult to cook with.

Or even better, you could let the seed mature and turn light brown, then carefully pull it off the plant. You might want a little bowl to put it in as you harvest.

Once you've collected all the seeds put them in an envelope and write on the front what they are and where they came from. You could decorate the envelope too with a picture of a hoverfly.

You can use this seed next year or, even better, you can send this to a friend so they can help the hoverflies too. And, just like that, you've become a SEED SAVER. Take a bow as this is one of the most important jobs in the world.

Save seeds for a better world!

Seed saved from your garden or pot will be slightly different from seed saved anywhere else in the world. We don't know what kind of seeds we will need in the future, but the more seed we have that is different and diverse the better prepared we will be.

Warning! Only try nectar from clover grown on a lawn that has not been sprayed or fertilised with chemicals.

Activity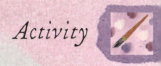

Clover

How to Taste Nectar

When I was a little kid, my mum and I used to lie on the lawn and drink as much clover nectar as we both could. It's not easy supping up nectar because clover is designed for bee tongues which are very, very thin and small compared to our mouths.

Very carefully pull one of the individual clover flowers (they look a bit like funnels) from the flower head and then very gently suck the bottom and see if there's any nectar.

A bee might have visited just before you and drunk it all, so sometimes you taste nothing, but other times you get a sweet hit of sugar. It's delicious but even if you drank all the clover on the lawn, it wouldn't even make up a whole teaspoon's worth!

ROOTS

Some roots don't grow in the soil but grow in the air, like the roots of many orchids. These roots have special cells on the outside that allow the root to capture moisture and food. This means the orchid can grow high up in the canopy of trees in the rainforest, where they can get more light.

Roots are like a plant's feet. They anchor the plant in the soil and at the same time they take up water so the plant can drink. A plant can't live for very long without its roots.

Because we don't see roots we don't think about them much, but they are so important to the plant. If the roots are happy the plant is happy, but if the roots are too cramped or too dry or too wet then the plant gets sad.

There are many different types of roots. Some roots act like storage for the plant over winter – carrots and parsnips are good examples of storage roots. They look after all the plant's food while it goes to sleep over winter.

The most magical thing roots do though is talk to each other. Plant roots are how plants communicate to each other and to all the other life in the soil. The plant roots send out chemicals telling nearby plants and all the tiny living things in the soil how they are feeling. They spend all day and all night saying things like 'I'm hungry', 'I like this rain' and 'I'm under attack from insects'.

Nematodes

The soil is full of tiny living things called microbes. Some of them are helpful to the plant and some aren't. When the plant's roots are under attack or haven't had enough rain, or too much sun, then the bad microbes move in and spoil things. When a plant's roots are happy it surrounds itself with friendly worms called nematodes.

The way we keep a plant's roots happy is to feed the soil. The best food for the soil is homemade compost (made from things like leftover dinner scraps,

Some roots creep along just below the surface of the soil. Blackberries and raspberries do this and mint loves to go running! It sends out roots in every direction as fast it can to establish new territory.

Some roots grow very slowly. The roots of oak trees take hundreds of years to grow to full size.

Making Art with Leaf Pounding

Fresh leaf-pounding is a very ancient art for decorating cloth that is used around the world. The Cherokee Nation of America use it to decorate quilts and in Japan it is quite an art.

All you need is some fresh leaves and flowers and some white material to pound onto.

How hard or soft you pound the plant materials affects how the picture comes out. If you pound very softly you will get all the detail of the flower or leaf, even each vein. If you pound very hard you get bold, smudgy colours and will end up with a more abstract piece of art. It may no longer look like a leaf or a flower, but it still has all the colour and energy of the plant.

See if you can make both a lifelike picture of the plant and an abstract one. Which one do you prefer, or maybe you like both? The great thing about being an artist is that you get to do whatever you want!

You will need:

- Something to act as a hammer — rubber hammers are best so ask your adult if they have one that they can help you use, but you could also use a large pebble from the garden or park
- A flat piece of thick wood to bash onto e.g. a spare plank of wood or a sturdy wooden chopping board, so long as you get your adult's permission to use it!
- Some white natural material: calico, linen, an old bed sheet or pillowcase, a hanky, old T-shirts
- Any fresh leaves and flowers that you like (but ask permission before picking anyone else's plants!) — the pot marigolds from pp. 40–41 are perfect

Activity

1 On top of your piece of wood, lay down the piece of white material that you want to decorate, place your leaf or flower on top of this and then lay down your spare piece of material on top of the leaf or flower.

2 Now carefully, with the guidance of your adult, use your hammer or pebble to start pounding the cloth until the colour of the plant starts to appear.

3 Once you have pounded all over the plant, peel back the top piece of material and remove your leaf or flower. You should be left with an imprint of some kind on your white material.

4 Once you've got the hang of this you can start to make your own art. You could create a picture of a woodland floor with lots of leaves, you could make a wildflower meadow or something really abstract and colourful.

Now you can start experimenting with pounding very softly or very hard. Which results do you prefer?

A note: If you wash the cloth the colour may run and will eventually fade.

73

Growing a Sweet Potato

Sweet potatoes originally come from Central America where they grow as rambling vines that have heart-shaped leaves.

The sweet potato that you eat is called a tuber and is an underground storage root. If you give it some water and light it will start to grow again.

Sweet potatoes don't do very well growing outside in our climate, so it's best to grow yours as a houseplant. If it's very happy it will grow really long stems. An ideal place to grow your sweet potato is on a shelf near a sunny window so the stems can trail down.

You will need:
- A sweet potato
- A big jam jar
- A big pot with drainage holes
- Water
- Toothpicks
- Compost
- A sunny, warm spot

1 Halfway down your sweet potato, stick in the three toothpicks at equal distance so that your sweet potato can sit on the rim of your jam jar.

2 Fill your jam jar with warm water. Place your sweet potato so that the pointy end sits in the water and the slightly rounder end pokes out of the jar.

3 Place the jar on a warm windowsill and top up the water if it starts to dry out. It's a good idea to replace the water if it starts to become cloudy.

Growing

4 It should take about two to three weeks for the sweet potato to start to sprout both leaves and roots.

5 When the roots hit the bottom of the jam jar and there are numerous leaves sprouting it is time to pot up the sweet potato into its proper home.

6 Choose a pot that is big enough to accommodate the roots without bending or folding them. The tuber needs to sit so that any sprouting leaves are not buried. Gently fill around the roots with compost until you reach the top of the pot.

Be patient, your sweet potato may take up to a month to sprout!

7 Now put your pot on a saucer so you can water it from its roots and sit it in a sunny place. The leaves won't like direct sunlight as they could burn.

The larger the pot the longer the vines will grow, so if you see roots coming out of the bottom of the drainage holes then it's time for a bigger container.

How to Make a Butterfly Happy

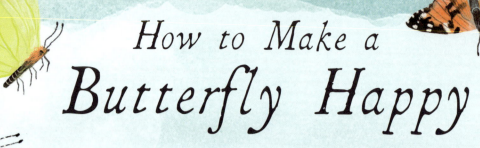

Butterflies have the longest tongues of any of our pollinators. Their tongues are so long they have to roll them up as they fly about or else they would flap about and get in the way!

These very long, thin tongues like to drink a certain kind of nectar. Nectar is made up of sugars and a thick nectar solution is a bit like honey. It would be really hard to drink honey through a straw! Plants know this so they dilute their nectar with water to make it runny, just like you dilute juice.

Because of their long tongues, butterflies need very weak nectar. Bees are greedy things and they'd drink all the nectar around, but some plants help butterflies to get their fair share because they have flowers that only the thin, long tongues of butterflies can get to. We call these butterfly plants.

Did you know butterflies taste with their feet, not their tongues?

Dame's violet

Greater knapweed

Growing

One of the most famous butterfly plants is the butterfly bush buddleia. You'll see bees have a go at getting some of the nectar, but the plant makes sure that deep in its tiny flowers there's always plenty that bee tongues can't reach.

Buddleia

You will need:

- Butterfly plant seeds: common knapweed, greater knapweed, field scabious, wild marjoram, dame's violet and teasel are all great and easy to grow
- A rake
- A watering can

You can either buy your seeds separately or in a wildflower mix. If you are growing in pots then wild marjoram and field scabious are your best bet.

WILD MARJORAM

FIELD SCABIOUS

Note for your adult:
The seed packet should say what size patch it is suitable for. If in doubt, double up the amount you want to sow to get a good distribution.

Common knapweed

Wild marjoram

Teasel

Field scabious

How to sow Butterfly Seeds

You need to sow these seeds on bare ground with no weeds or grass. Sow them in September or March, April or the beginning of May.

1. Scatter the seeds across the ground. Some of these seeds are so small it is easy for them to all fall in the same place. To stop this happening, you can mix the seed in with a little sand – this will help you see where you are scattering the seeds.

If you sowed your seeds in autumn, then they should start flowering by June. If you sowed your seeds in March/April/May then they will flower from August to September.

2. Gently rake over the seeds so they settle in and give them a good drink of water from a watering can.

If it hasn't rained after a week, you will need to water the whole patch again. The seeds should come up after a couple of weeks.

See how many butterflies (and bees) visit. Perhaps you could make a chart of all the different butterflies?

Butterfly spotter

- ○ Comma
- ○ Brimstone
- ○ Orange-tip
- ○ Small tortoiseshell
- ○ Small white
- ○ Peacock
- ○ Small blue
- ○ Red admiral
- ○ Chequered skipper
- ○ Green-veined white
- ○ Painted lady
- ○ Common blue

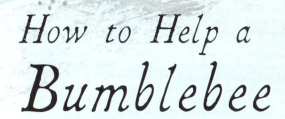

How to Help a Bumblebee

A bumblebee works very hard all day long pollinating plants, but sometimes the flowers are far apart and it gets tired or it's too early in the spring and there aren't enough flowers, or sometimes it just gets lost on its way home and runs out of energy.

The poor bumblebee feels exhausted and starts to get confused. You often see these bees on the floor or pavement wandering around too tired to fly.

You can help the bumblebee out by giving it a quick meal of sugar. Watch how quickly it gets all its energy back and flies off!

You will need:
- A teaspoon
- An 1/8th of a teaspoon (that's a tiny pinch) of sugar
- A little warm water

1. Bees don't drink a lot so you just need to dissolve the sugar in the water on the teaspoon.

2. Take the teaspoon to the bee and place it near their head. Bumblebees can smell sugar so it'll move to the teaspoon and take a drink.

If you look carefully, you'll see its tongue lapping up the sweet drink and then it will start to shake its body, which is like it starting up its flight engine – and woosh!

Off it'll fly.

Grow Your Own Lentil Farm

You can create your own micro windowsill farm using dried lentils, mung beans or chickpeas from your kitchen cupboard.

Lentils

1. Fill the seed tray with compost and decide where you want your pond to go. If you are using a mirror for the pond then you can just nudge it into the compost. If you are using a small yoghurt pot then you need to bury it so that you can't see the edges. Then when you've finished your farm you can fill the pond up with water for the animals to drink.

You will need:

- A seed tray (a large takeaway tray from the recycling will do)
- Compost
- Dried lentils (brown or green whole lentils are best as split lentils are no longer a whole seed so can't sprout), mung beans or chickpeas
- Plastic farm figurines – a farmer, farm animals (or dinosaurs, unicorns ... whatever you want!)
- A small mirror or a small yoghurt pot to make a pond
- A tray without holes or DIY tray made of aluminium foil
- A watering can

The soil in your seed tray doesn't need to be flat – you can make a hill on one side if you wish. Don't make it too close to the edge of the seed tray though or else you might have a landslide!

Chickpeas   Mung beans   Growing

2 Now take a small handful of lentils (or mung beans or chickpeas if using these) and plant up your fields and hill. You just need to gently push each lentil into the compost so it is slightly buried.

3 Around your fields you could put a fence (you could make this out of Lego if you don't have a farm animal set) and a gate, or you could allow your farm animals to roam wherever they like.

Your seeds should sprout in about four days and you will need to water your farm at least every other day or whenever the soil dries out.

Your farm will need a tray underneath it to catch water. If you don't have one, ask an adult to help you make one using aluminium foil.

4 Place your seed tray on a windowsill or near a window somewhere warm, as lentils like it around 20 degrees Celsius.

5 Now using your watering can, gently water in your farm. Remember both lentils and animals prefer gentle watering that's like the rain rather than a big gush of water which will definitely cause a landslide!

Make sure your farm gets plenty of light so your crops grow good and strong.

Growing Microgreens

Microgreens are very tiny salads. They are the seedling leaves of lettuce, herbs and other delightful things that pack a flavour punch even though they are really small.

Microgreens are grown just like pea shoots. One of my favourite ways to grow microgreens is to use recycled plastic takeaway trays. You can either raid your kitchen cupboard for seeds or use some of your leftover ones from other growing projects. Here's some suggestions:

Seeds to Try for Microgreens

From your kitchen cupboard:

Popcorn kernels: super sweet and delicious

Dried coriander seeds: these will grow super quick into a herby treat

Dried chickpeas: these grow very quickly (you need to cook the young leaves just like spinach for them to taste best)

Fennel seeds: these grow into tiny fairy fronds of sweet liquorice-tasting leaves

From your seed store:

Watercress seeds: spicy hot and sweet!

Radish seeds: the leaves are super spicy and hot, so you'll have to be brave to try them

Broccoli seeds: super delicious and very sweet leaves

Beetroot seeds: the leaves are earthy and sweet

Lettuce seeds: these make soft and tender leaves

Spinach seeds: spinach leaves are everyone's favourite

Growing

How to Grow Microgreens

You will need:
- An adult
- A plastic takeaway tray and lid (the lid will act as both a greenhouse for your seeds and then when they're up it can be used as a saucer below your tray to catch water)
- Compost
- Seeds (any of the seeds suggested will do)
- Watering can
- Scissors

1 First you need to make some drainage holes in the bottom of your plastic tray. Ask your adult to do this for you (see p.46).

2 Fill your tray ¾ full with compost and water in well. You can either use your watering can or fill your kitchen washing-up bowl with some water, sit the tray in it and let it soak up.

3 Sow your seeds thickly but evenly over the compost. Try to make sure the seeds are not sitting on top of each other.

4 Cover big seeds such as coriander, beetroot, spinach and popcorn with compost, but little seeds such as radish, watercress and lettuce don't need covering up.

5 Put a clear lid or plastic bag over the container and wait.

6 Most greens will be up in four or five days and you can start harvesting once they are 3 cm high. It is best to use scissors to harvest. Remember: once you've cut the plant it won't grow again.

7 Don't throw away the compost once you've harvested. Add a thin new layer of fresh compost and sow again. You can keep doing this at least another three times to top up your supply of microgreens.

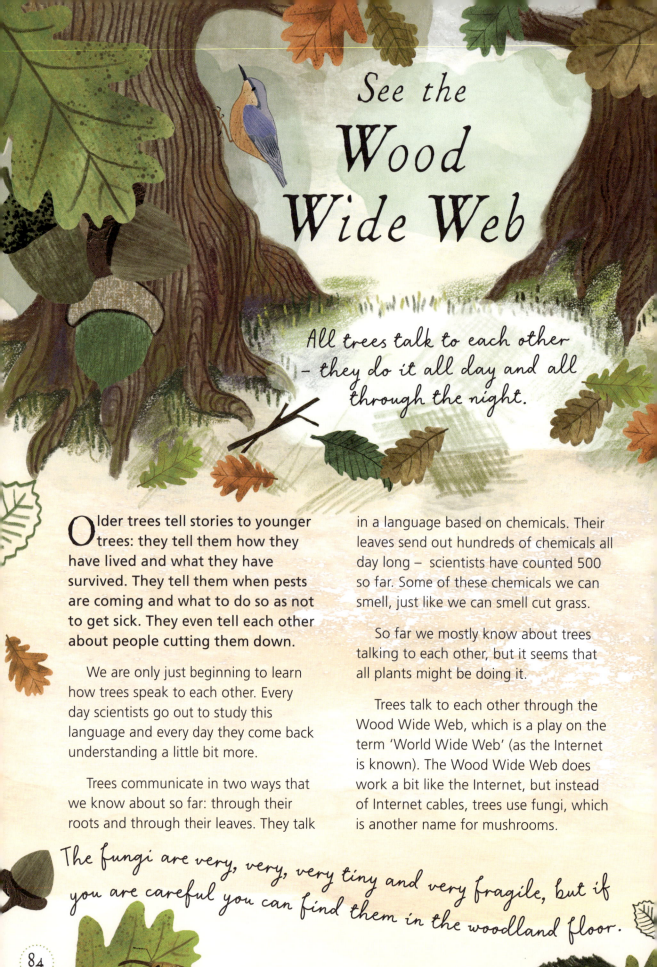

See the Wood Wide Web

All trees talk to each other – they do it all day and all through the night.

Older trees tell stories to younger trees: they tell them how they have lived and what they have survived. They tell them when pests are coming and what to do so as not to get sick. They even tell each other about people cutting them down.

We are only just beginning to learn how trees speak to each other. Every day scientists go out to study this language and every day they come back understanding a little bit more.

Trees communicate in two ways that we know about so far: through their roots and through their leaves. They talk in a language based on chemicals. Their leaves send out hundreds of chemicals all day long – scientists have counted 500 so far. Some of these chemicals we can smell, just like we can smell cut grass.

So far we mostly know about trees talking to each other, but it seems that all plants might be doing it.

Trees talk to each other through the Wood Wide Web, which is a play on the term 'World Wide Web' (as the Internet is known). The Wood Wide Web does work a bit like the Internet, but instead of Internet cables, trees use fungi, which is another name for mushrooms.

The fungi are very, very, very tiny and very fragile, but if you are careful you can find them in the woodland floor.

Experiment

Oak tree

Fungi

You will need:

- An adult
- A magnifying glass
- A woodland or group of trees

These fungi have a really good friendship with tree roots. In return for connecting one tree with its neighbour's roots and its neighbour with the tree next door and so on, the fungi are paid in sugar and other nutrients from the tree. The more the fungi are fed the further they can reach in connecting the tree with all its neighbours.

1. Choose a tree and find a spot very close to it with lots of leaf litter on the ground. Now, with your fingers, carefully pull back the soil just below the surface.

2. With your magnifying glass look closely at the soil. Can you see any white bits that look like cotton wool? Well, that's the fungi's cables connecting the trees together. If you spot this then you have seen the Wood Wide Web! What do you think the trees are saying today? I bet they're talking about the weather …

Warning!

Some fungi are poisonous so make sure you don't touch or pull up any fungi you see in the leaf litter. Ask your adult to help you find a patch of soil that is free of fungi and always wash your hands properly after this activity.

How to be a Bee

Did you know you can act just like a bee and buzz around the garden pollinating flowers?

It may sound silly but it's a serious job. I have a friend who works for Kew Gardens in London and she spends all day going around pollinating plants.

Kew Gardens has plants from all around the world, and some of these plants are very rare and come from places where the plant's home has disappeared. People might have built over it or it might have been burnt or flooded. Kew Gardens looks after these plants until their homes can be restored.

Kew is very good at creating the same environment as the plant's home but it can't bring the plant's pollinators into the greenhouses to live. It doesn't have hummingbirds, bats or tropical bees, wasps or big fat beetles.

So my friend's job is to go around taking the pollen from one plant and putting it on the female part of another flower to make seeds. Then these seeds are stored away until the plant can go home again.

Now it's your turn to be a pollinator!

You can only pollinate a tomato flower with tomato flower pollen or a courgette with pollen from another courgette flower. You can't pollinate a tomato with a courgette or a rose with a sweet pea because they don't like each other's pollen.

I Choose a flower and check there aren't any bees already doing the work for you. If the flower is free, take out your brush and jiggle it around over the pollen.

You will need:

- A soft small paintbrush
- Some plants in flower
- Eagle eyesight (pollen is very small!)

Raspberry

Activity

2 Now take the brush away very carefully and have a look at what colour pollen you have. Most pollen is yellowy-orange or yellow, but dandelion pollen is bright orange-red, raspberry pollen is grey, oriental poppy pollen is almost black and red deadnettle pollen is dark blood red!

3 You can tap the pollen off onto a white sheet of paper. If you do this with a few different flowers then you can see how many different colours you can find.

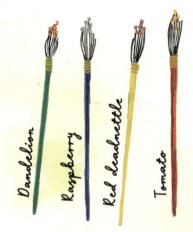

Dandelion · Raspberry · Red deadnettle · Tomato

4 But if you want to be a good bee you must take the pollen you've collected on your brush and drop it off onto another flower so it can be pollinated and turn into seeds.

5 Carefully taking your brush loaded with pollen, go to a different flower of the same kind and tap the pollen off onto the sticky stigma (this is at the end of the long pointy bit that sticks out from the centre of the flower). It is sticky to catch the grains of pollen and start fertilisation.

stigma

Red deadnettle

We have the bees and other pollinators to thank for so much of our food, from fruits such as apples, pears, raspberries, strawberries and tomatoes, to veggies such as aubergines and peppers, and even the cocoa in chocolate.

Even the milk we drink from cows is thanks to the bees. Cows eat plants such as clover to make good, healthy milk and the bees pollinate the clover flowers. In fact, we'd only be eating grasses if it wasn't for all the pollinators, so let's be kind to the bees!

STEMS

The stem is a plant's motorway system. It's the part that takes the water and nutrients from the roots to the leaves and flowers and then back down again. All day long the cells in the stem are transporting goods around the plant.

They also help the plant to stay upright or creep along the ground depending on whether the plant is the sort that wants to stand up straight like a tree or scramble along like a blackberry.

Some stems wrap themselves around things so the plant can grow upright. A runner bean does this by swirling around a cane so that it can grow up into the sun.

Some stems, such as blackberries and roses, have vicious thorns. Thorns help protect the plant from hungry animals eating it. No one wants a mouthful of thorns! But sometimes the thorns are helping the plant to climb up things, hooking themselves on so they can climb ever taller.

If a thorn tip points down then it's there to help hook the plant up in the world. If the tip points upwards or just outwards, then the plant is using this as a warning: 'Don't come near me and definitely don't eat me!'

Some stems are huge, like the trunk of an oak tree, and some are wispy thin, like that of a blade of grass. Big stems, like tree trunks, tend to take a long time to grow so grand. You can tell the age of a tree by counting the rings inside the tree. Each ring represents a year in the life of a tree.

At the top of the stem is the primary growing point. This is the part that grows new cells so that the plant can get taller and fatter.

Some plants have sticky hooks on their stems, like on the stem of sticky willy, the hedge plant. You can play a fun game of sticking sticky willy to the back of people's jumpers when they aren't looking.

Using Kitchen Scraps to Grow New Plants

Did you know your kitchen scraps can become new plants? Many vegetables will re-sprout with just a little water and their new growth is soft, tender and tasty. See which one you like eating most.

For beetroot, turnips, swedes and carrots you need just the top bit of the vegetable where the leaves would grow. You need about 2-5 cm of top, which is usually the bit that is cut off for cooking.

For stuff like celery, onions, spring onions, leeks, lettuce and even pak choi, you need the base of the vegetable. Ask your adult to cut 5-8 cm off the base.

With lettuce and onions, you need to put the cut-off base in a pot of damp soil. You can just place the base onto the soil rather than burying it.

For all your other veg tops and bases, sit them in a little water in a saucer on a sunny windowsill and after a few days you'll start to see new growth appear.

Growing

Grow Neon Pink Beetroot in the Dark

Now if you're feeling really adventurous you can try growing some of the beetroot tops in the dark! This is known as 'forcing' the vegetable because you are forcing it to grow without light, and this changes the colour of the leaves.

If you want lots of leaves use a whole beetroot but if you just want a few leaves then you can use a beetroot top.

You will need:

- A pot just large enough to hold the beetroot
- Compost
- Water
- A much larger pot that will cover your beetroot pot
- Some masking tape or newspaper

1 Plant up your beetroot in the smaller pot with some compost. The top of the beetroot needs to be sitting on the surface of the soil. Water in the compost and sit the pot on a saucer.

2 Now, cover the drainage holes of the large pot with tape or by stuffing some newspaper in the bottom. It's very important that no light gets in.

3 Place the large upturned pot over the planted-up beetroot.

4 The beetroot needs to be somewhere warm, but not where it will dry out (so not too close to a radiator).

After a week, check to see how it's growing. What colour are the leaves? Because the leaves are growing in the dark, they won't produce green pigment. Instead they will be yellow or even white!

How to Make a Willow Star Wand

Willow is a magical tree and we've been using it for a very long time as a medicine. The painkiller aspirin originally came from willow, and it's also used as a building material. For centuries we made all our shopping baskets out of it!

Willow is often found growing near water and this means that its bark is very watery and flexible, allowing it to bend in the wind. This bendiness makes it perfect for weaving: we can make circles for baskets or bend it into hoops, but even better we can make willow stars.

We only weave with willow in the winter when the leaves have fallen off the tree. You'll often find willow growing along riverbanks, in parks and even car parks. You could ask your local park keeper if you could have a few branches.

If you can't find free willow, you could also look for dogwood (this often has bright red stems in winter) or you can buy willow stems for weaving. You may need to soak them first to make them bendy.

1 Ask your adult to cut the willow stems as close to the base as possible using the secateurs.

Warning!
Make sure not to poke yourself, or anyone else, in the eye.

2 Bend the willow stem carefully in half, making sure not to completely crack it in two. This bend will be the top of the star.

You will need:
- Long, thin straight willow stems, at least 1 m long and about the thickness of a pencil
- Some gloves (it might be cold)
- Secateurs (and an adult to help)
- String or ribbon
- PVA glue

Activity

Now bend the rest of the stem into the shape of a star by following this diagram:

3. You can tie the bottom of the wand with some string or ribbon. If you want to, you could also decorate it with buttons, autumn leaves, tree seeds and moss using PVA glue.

Note: *If you plant your wand in a pot it will most likely sprout new leaves to become a tree.*

Once your willow star wand is finished you could cast a magic spell over it so that it can spread even more magic.

Here's a simple spell:

*Hello world, hello willow
Thanks for bending double
With so little trouble!
Now I've made you into a wand,
With this magic, here I cast
A spell to make all willow last.*

Index

A
air 35
air plants 26, 27
apples 55
avocados 30, 31, 32

B
basil 38
bees 19, 39, 57, 62, 66, 69, 78, 79, 86, 87
  bumblebees 79
beetles 20, 39, 57
beetroot 50, 82, 83, 90, 91
bird of Paradise flower 19
blackberries 71, 88
broad beans 10
broccoli 19, 82
buddleia (butterfly bush) 77
buds 52, 53
butterflies 17, 19, 57, 76, 77, 78

C
cacti 45
calendula 39
Calendula officianalis (pot marigold or common marigold) 33, 39, 40
carbon dioxide 11, 45
carnations 37
carrots 70, 90
celery 36, 37, 90
cells 27, 28, 88, 89
chickpeas 78, 79, 81
Chinese cabbage 36, 37
chives 39
chlorophyll 45
chrysanthemums 37
clover 69
coco de mer 35
common jasmine 60
communication, plant 70, 84
compost 8, 10, 11, 12, 13, 14, 15, 22, 29, 32, 60, 65, 66, 75, 80, 83, 91
coriander 66, 67, 68, 82, 83
courgettes 39

D
dandelions 38, 42, 52, 53, 87
  dandelion pancakes 42
Datura 19
deadnettle 87
Dianthus barbatus (sweet william) 57
dogwood 92
drainage 46
dye 50, 51

E
earwigs 39
edible flowers 38, 39, 40, 42
eggs 19
energy 45
equipment 8

F
fennel 81
fertilisation 19
field scabious 77
flowers 17, 18–19, 24, 25, 38–39, 40–41, 42, 43, 52, 58–59, 60, 66, 69, 72, 76, 79, 86, 87
foraging 16, 52
'forcing' 91
frogs 57
fruit 30
fungi 84, 85

G
gardens 56–57, 66, 86
garlic mustard 17
germination 10, 31, 34, 63
Geum urbanum (herb bennet) 54, 55
grasses 19, 89
grit 29

H
hairs 65
hand trowels *see* trowels
hedges 17
herb bennet 54, 55
hoes 9
hoverflies 66, 67, 68

I
insects 20, 24, 57, 66

K
kitchen scraps 90–91

L
labelling 11, 33
ladybirds 20
leaf pounding 72–73
leaves 13, 14, 16, 17, 20, 23, 27, 28, 29, 32, 35, 36, 37, 44–45, 53, 63, 65, 67, 72, 75, 81, 82, 83, 84, 90, 91
leeks 90
lentil farm 78–79
lentils 78, 79
lettuce 82, 90
light 10, 35
lunch 22
loo roll tubes 47
Lonicera periclymenum (wild honeysuckle) 59

M
marigolds 10, 33, 39, 40, 43
medicine 40, 92
microbes 71
microgreens 82–83
minibeasts 20
mint 71
moths 57, 58, 59, 60
mung beans 78, 79

N
nasturtiums 10, 38, 40
nectar 19, 39, 57, 62, 69, 77
nectaries 24, 76
nematodes 71
newspaper 13
nutrients 85, 88

O
oak 71, 89
onions 90
orange cheese sauce 43
orchids 34, 70
ovaries 18, 19
oxygen 35, 45

P
pak choi 90
paper 48, 49, 50
  wildflower seedpaper 48, 49, 50
parsnip pea-shooter 62–64
parsnips 62, 63, 64, 70
peas 10, 22, 23, 47, 64
peat-free compost *see* compost
perfume 24, 25
perlite 29
petals 18, 24, 41, 43
photosynthesis 45
pips 30, 31, 32
  see also seeds
pistils 18
plant labels 9, 33, 63
plant names 33

plant pots 8, 10, 12, 13, 14, 15, 32, 41, 46, 47
pollen 18, 19, 24, 39, 62, 86, 87
pollination 18, 86, i87
pollinators 19, 24, 48, 57, 62, 65, 76, 86
pollution 16
ponds 57
popcorn 82, 83
poppies 87
potting on 14
prayer plants 45

R
rabbits 53
radish 82, 83
Rafflesia arnoldii 18
rakes 9
raspberries 71, 87
red onion 50
rocket 38
runner beans 10, 88
roots 7, 11, 13, 14, 27, 28, 29, 31, 34, 36, 45, 52–53, 54, 55, 65, 70–71, 74, 75, 84, 85, 88
roses 88

S
scent 24
secateurs 8
seedlings 8, 11, 12, 13, 14, 15, 34, 35, 41, 47, 56, 57, 63, 67, 81
seeds 7, 10, 18, 19, 22, 30, 34–35, 40, 41, 48, 49, 50, 58,

59, 63, 66, 68, 77, 78, 81
seed coats 34, 35
seed saving 68
seed trays 8, 10, 78
sowing seeds 7, 10, 34, 40, 58, 59
sheep's sorrel 17
shoots 22, 23, 28
slugs 56, 57
soil 40, 41, 70, 71
snails 57
spiders 20
spinach 82, 83
spines 45
spring onions 90
squirting cucumbers 34
stamens 18
stems 28, 36, 37, 64, 65, 88–89, 92
sticky willy 89
stigmas 18, 19
succulents 28, 29, 44
sugar 45, 79
sunflowers 10
swedes 90
sweet potatoes 74, 75
sweet william 57

T
taking up water 36
thinning 7
thorns 88
toads 57
tomatoes 12, 13, 15, 65
trees 32, 84, 85, 89, 92

Tropaeolum majus (nasturtium) 40
trowels 9
tubers 74, 75
turnips 90

V
vegetable ink dye 50–51
vegetables 90
vegetative propagation 28
Venus flytraps 45
violets 38

W
water 34, 36, 45, 61
watercress 82, 83
watering cans 8, 11, 61
watering in 7, 11, 12, 65, 81, 83, 91
wild honeysuckle 59
wild marjoram 77
wildflowers 48, 49, 50, 52
  see also flowers
willow 92, 93
  willow star wand 92–93
wind 19, 24
Wolffia angusta 19
Wood Wide Web 84, 85

X
xylem 36, 37

To Jamesy, Hester and Arthur
A.F

For my two wild flowers, Florence & Henry x
H.G

The Royal Botanic Gardens, Kew is world famous as a scientific organisation and for its stunning landscapes at Kew Gardens and at Wakehurst, Kew's Wild Botanic Garden in the Sussex High Weald. Wakehurst is home to Kew's Millennium Seed Bank, which houses and protects seeds from the world's most substantial and diverse collection of threatened and useful wild plants. Your purchase supports Kew's vital work around the world – protecting biodiversity, saving plants and fungi that might one day save us.

www.kew.org

BLOOMSBURY CHILDREN'S BOOKS
Bloomsbury Publishing Plc
50 Bedford Square, London, WC1B 3DP, UK
29 Earlsfort Terrace, Dublin 2

BLOOMSBURY, BLOOMSBURY CHILDREN'S BOOKS and the Diana logo
are trademarks of Bloomsbury Publishing Plc
First published in Great Britain 2021 by Bloomsbury Publishing Plc
Text copyright © Alys Fowler, 2021

Illustrations copyright © Heidi Griffiths, 2021
Alys Fowler and Heidi Griffiths have asserted their rights under the Copyright, Designs and Patents Act, 1988,
to be identified as Author and Illustrator of this work

All rights reserved.
No part of this publication may be reproduced or transmitted in any form or by any means, electronic or mechanical, including photocopying, recording, or any information storage or retrieval system, without prior permission in writing from the publishers

A catalogue record for this book is available from the British Library

ISBN: 9781526619105

2 4 6 8 10 9 7 5 3 1

FSC
www.fsc.org
MIX
Paper from
responsible sources
FSC® C020056

Printed and bound in China by Leo Paper Products, Heshan, Guangdong
To find out more about our authors and books visit www.bloomsbury.com and sign up for our newsletters

One bee was rescued during the making of this book